BILLY CHAPATA

flawers

Copyright © 2016 by Billy Chapata

All rights reserved.

ISBN 978-1-329-92737-7

flawers

what are these things you call flaws? are they parts of yourself that you don't admire? parts of yourself that you don't understand? parts of yourself you don't like? parts of yourself that you feel you need to change?

or are your flaws simply things that other people do not accept? parts of you that individuals and society cannot accept because they don't understand? parts of yourself that people have looked down upon because they haven't quite grasped your entire being? parts of yourself that people turn away because they can't comprehend the traits you possess?

your little intricate habits, emotional traits and patterns of behavior are what make you the truly unique individual you are. take away all these things and you erase your very essence, you tarnish you aura, you spoil your uniqueness, you fail to exist.

why would you want to do that? why would you want to change or remove something that makes you stand out beautifully amongst the crowd? the very puzzle piece that makes you, you? it may not seem like it, but there are people out there who will find these things beautiful. people who will accept you the way you are, unconditionally. people who don't want to change a single thing about you. people who don't see your flaws, as flaws. people who will admire your imperfections as something that is irreplaceable and divine.

understand that your flaws, are not flaws. they are things you can grow from, things you can learn from, things you don't necessarily need to change, things that you don't have to be ashamed of, things that you can embrace.

don't be afraid of your flaws, don't shy away, gravitate towards them, place them on a pedestal, and tell the world "this is me, and I won't change a single thing to suit anything or anyone". let your flaws be your flowers.

"you just need someone

that will make you realize

that your flaws are just

undiscovered beauties within you."

- billy chapata

impatience

what soul celebrates at the thought of waiting?

the thought of waiting for something to happen?

the thought of waiting for someone to come through with what your soul craves or what your heart desires?

no matter how lucrative the end result seems to be, the thought of waiting for a particular event or peculiar thing is never the most appetizing prospect. we're only human for feeling this way, our souls itch at the prospect of getting our hearts desire. whether that be a physical object, something intangible, or just a feeling, the heart wants what the heart wants, and these are urges we cannot easily reject.

perhaps, impatience is not a flaw but a realization of your self-worth. you know what you deserve and you crave it now, there is no wrong in that. embrace that feeling, this is not a flaw.

"you're highly flammable.

it only takes one

word to set you off."

- *billy chapata*

temper/anger

situations, people, life. things that all tend to get the better of us in certain instances. the urge to shout at the top of your lungs so loud that you can cause the amazon rainforest to tremble at the mere intensity of your voice and feelings. the urge to release all this pent up frustration on a particular person or a particular thing.

this is normal.

we all have times when the intensity of our situations or emotions reach the maximum point of no return. a point when our boiling point has been reached at such a profuse rate. a point that leaves us helpless with no option but just to lash out, intentionally or unintentionally.

you may just be hot blooded and passionate about things that don't go your way or situations you wish you could alter or change, but that's the irony of it all. the fiery, hot, intense individuals are the ones who are the most passionate. passion is a beautiful thing, just learn to channel that passion through less anger, and more love.

temper is not a flaw, but a flower. something you can grow and learn from.

"to the world,

you seem so

cold hearted.

you have so

much love to give,

but haven't found

a soul that

deserves it."

- ***billy chapata***

hopeless romantic

who doesn't want to feel love?

who doesn't want to be loved?

who doesn't want to tangle themselves in a beautiful romance that would make your favorite novel or romantic movie jealous?

a romance that lasts for decades with a person who you cherish more than the clouds that admire the peak of a mountain top?

sadly, at times life never goes as planned. love, never goes as planned. we try repeatedly, and indulge ourselves in all these connections that curiously always seem to fail. and as human beings we tend to search for answers at this point.

why does it never work?

why is all my love never reciprocated?

why do i indulge myself in connections that i know are doomed to begin with?

is there something wrong with me? am i a hopeless romantic?

the problem, is never you. you have so much love to give. love that comes with no conditions but just an abundance of purity and intensity. but you have to learn patience. not everyone deserves your love. having all this love to give is not a flaw. a day will come when someone who can handle your warmth and grasp your love in its fullest entirety, will arrive at your hearts doorstep. let your love be your flower, and wait patiently for someone who is willing to water and keep that flower safe in their hearts garden.

"it's okay to be alone,

it's okay to enjoy solitude,

it's okay to enjoy silence.

this is not insanity,

this is wisdom.

- *billy chapata*

anti-social

there is an obsession that plagues our world and different societies that entails that anyone who keeps to themselves is anti-social. if you don't like interacting with others, "you're not a nice person", "you're either sad or upset", or you aren't socially fit to be around other people. this lack of empathy from other individuals should never cause you to feel any guilt.

what's wrong with keeping to myself?

what's wrong with staying indoors and indulging in my own company?

what's wrong with remaining silent and choosing to keep my thoughts to myself?

does this make you anti-social, or more self aware? you don't have to interact with everything to be whole. at times, it's the very people who we are encouraged to interact with that drain us and cause us to feel empty. why chase a feeling that you know you do not want, just so you can fit into societies norms?

maybe you just understand your self-worth. you value your time and your space, but they don't, so you keep to yourself?

whatever your reasons for deciding to indulge in solitude, be unapologetic in your actions. there is nothing wrong with wanting to be away from the distractions and noise people may present. this is not a flaw, but a flower. flowers don't need to be around other flowers to grow. they just bloom.

"the moon

has an uncanny

way of stripping

the mind naked.

a temptress

that seduces you,

leaving you over-thinking

at night."

- billy chapata

over-thinker & over-analyzer

your mind is flooded with different things and sometimes it becomes overwhelming. things that you're not even sure of how they found themselves in your mind in the first place.

thoughts that linger in the corners of your mind like glitter from a birthday party ten years ago.

it can be the most irrelevant thought, or a thought so raw that your brain bleeds just at the prospect of it. this thought causes you to worry, get scared, get anxious or stress out unnecessarily.

while this may seem like a horrible thing, there is a silver lining in it all. to think about things so deeply is not a flaw, but a gift. you're in tune with your environment, you're aware, you're alive.

so many poor souls roam this earth unable to think of the slightest thing.

why?

because their experiences have made them so numb to the point that they are incapable of even fathoming the most shallow or deep thought.

embrace the fact that you're able to think so intensely, embrace the fact that you're analytical about a lot of things that happen in your life. being able to think as much is beautiful. you don't always have to go with the flow of life. sometimes the more thought out things turn out to be the most golden.

"you deserve clarity.

you deserve love that doesn't

cause you confusion or pain.

you deserve requited love.

know what you deserve."

- billy chapata

unlovable

sometimes failed connections leave us with more questions than answers and leave us feeling inadequate and undesirable. our failed connections can bring us to a point where we feel like there is something wrong with us.

am i too demanding?

am i not good enough?

do i care too much?

do i show too much, too early?

we end up summing up all these questions and coming to the conclusion that perhaps we are just unlovable. that our "flaws", preferences or ideas on love are way too unrealistic for anyone to accept, and that we can't be loved the way that we feel we should be loved.

since when was there a problem with having standards or being yourself when indulging in a connection?

maybe it's not a case of being unlovable, but a case of people not going the extra mile for you. people not going the distance that you deserve to be met at. you know your worth, you understand what you need to progress romantically, but you frequently find yourself at crossroads with the other person because they can't quite grasp that. this is not a flaw, but a flower. very few know what's best for them, but in all you do there is a tone of understanding within. wait for what you deserve.

"release and detox

from the poisons of

grudges and animosity.

you gain nothing by holding'

on to energy that

is not conducive."

- ***billy chapata***

too kind or too soft

sometimes we put up with things that we don't deserve because deep down it is the natural feeling that resonates within us to show a person kindness even though that's the last thing they deserve from us. we find ourselves feeling a deep inner conflict, because we want to love ourselves but also show that love outwards.

you let grudges go easily?

you forgive those who hurt you?

you're nice to those who don't reciprocate that kindness?

so what? is it such a bad thing to respond to bad with goodness? to show warmth in a world full of so much coldness? there is no such thing as being too kind or too nice. people like you are rare, something that we have to look around for deeply because there are more bitter than happy people in the world.

you want peace of mind and no burdens placed upon your soul, and that is admirable. this is no flaw, but a flower each one of us should have within us.

"don't change parts of

who you are to accommodate

someone else's emotions

actions or habits.

don't be disloyal to yourself."

- *billy chapata*

indifference & apathy

to feel different. is this a curse or blessing?

some would make you feel as if this is such a terrible thing and that you should be a little more empathetic to their situations and whatever hardships they are going through.

perhaps, you feel a little bad that you feel this way and wish you could sum up all the interest in your bones to show a little more concern about these things that people are going through.

but you don't. you just cannot help yourself to really gravitate to the issues at hand. is this a bad thing? absolutely not. you're human, not a robot. you cannot simply react in a particular manner because it is deemed socially or morally correct. you are you, and nothing can change that about you.

you feel indifferent for a reason. you're not here to be anyone's machine. you weren't built to understand anyone, but yourself.

perhaps it is brought about by the sheer lack of how relatable whatever the situation is? or perhaps your own nonchalance? or perhaps it is because you have your own issues to worry about?

to feel this way is not bad. you concern yourself with things that your soul gravitates towards and you reject the things that you do not resonate with. if only more people were the same. this is a flower, not a flaw.

"sometimes the vibes

are realer

when you're alone."

- *billy chapata*

abandonment issues

being alone is the hardest pill to swallow. feeling like everything that comes into your life will disappoint you or disappear at some stage is the scariest and most painful state of mind to be in.

this feeling can cause us not to trust.

not to be optimistic.

not to be happy.

it is a state of mind that is not easy to escape from. it's like being stuck in a prison alone behind bars without a key to release you from your captivity. but you cannot sit there, wallowing in your loneliness blaming yourself for feeling the way you do.

whatever situation you encountered or experienced brought you to this place you now occupy, and it is understandable that darkness can consume you to the point where you struggle to see the intention in people's faces. but there is always light at the end of the tunnel. someone will come in with a key, unlocking you from that prison, taking your hand with every intention of staying. it may not seem like it currently, but time will reveal all.

take your time when opening your heart. take deep breaths. be hopeful. let the past experiences be flowers you can grow from. lessons you can take into the future. lessons of strength, courage, and resilience. you will be okay.

"you are beautiful,

you are divine,

know what you're worth."

- billy chapata

entitlement

what do you deserve?

why do you deserve it?

when do you deserve it?

is it not relative? subjective?

to feel a sense of entitlement is not as bad as some people would have you make out. people love to paint this picture of a spoilt, needy, demanding person in distress who feels they deserve things that they don't.

but who are they to tell you what you deserve? are you not the person feeling these vibrations and impulses to receive what your heart desires and soul craves for? how can another human being be judgmental of what you feel you deserve?

what you feel you deserve is merely a reflection of your own thoughts and no one has the right to tell you how to think. it is a beautiful thing to draw a line in the sand and tell yourself that this is what you deserve and you will not stumble for someone else's perceptions of what they feel you're worth.

there is nothing wrong with having standards and feeling like you are entitled to what you're entitled to, especially if it affects your happiness. this just indicates an abundance of self love and self respect. these are flowers some wish they had. don't throw them away for someone not willing to understand your worth.

"you owe it to yourself

to be happy.

don't let your joy depend

on another soul."

- billy chapata

codependent

are you able to exist alone? or do you need another soul to validate your existence? would whatever essence you embody completely vanish if the person you place all your existence in disappears?

it's okay, to feel the need to rely on another soul for growth and comfort. we're human, sometimes are own warmth isn't enough to keep us alive when cold times come along. sometimes the presence of another soul elevates us to new heights that we could ordinarily not reach on our own.

but what happens if the person you put all your stock in fails to meet your requirements?

will you still be the same?

or will something drastically change?

will you be unhappy?

understand that there is nothing wrong with leaning on someone for support, love and comfort. but also understand that it is important to be able to sustain on your own. it is important to be your own cushion that you can fall in for comfort when no one else is around. when you place your foundation in an individual, when they crumble, your world crumbles too. make sure your world exists without the need of another soul, and you will truly grow with or without their presence. let this be a flower, not a flaw.

"you're human.

allow yourself to be

upset, sad or angry.

allow yourself to feel.

allow yourself to grow

from bad experiences.

- billy chapata

self-critical

often times we find ourselves targeting within. putting a target on our souls and taking multiple shots with a loaded shotgun because we are unsatisfied or unhappy with a certain element we encompass.

we feel we should do better, can do better, be better.

but why do we feel this way?

is it something we just feel boiling at the depths of our guts?

or is it because of this certain rapport the media and society has built of what is deemed acceptable and what is not?

we are creatures of habit and sometimes we get in a system of constantly abusing ourselves by being so critical of ourselves. there is nothing wrong with being hard on yourself, nothing wrong with striving for better, nothing wrong with analyzing ourselves and measuring how much we've grown.

but when it becomes a habit, it becomes unhealthy. live your life. stop looking at yourself so much and stop constantly looking for ways to improve something that is so perfect already. stop measuring your beauty or characteristics to other individuals. flowers don't care about the other flowers growing in the garden, they just bloom. bloom unapologetically. be easy on yourself, be gentle with yourself, be loving with yourself, be the most beautiful flower in the garden.

"you fell in love

and immediately

fell out of love

with yourself.

that's when i

knew the one you

love wasn't loving you

the way you deserve.

- *billy chapata*

<u>lover of the undeserving</u>

all this love. all this beautiful, vibrant and radiant love you have to give. love that cannot be compared to anything. love so pure and intense that it puts a poets thoughts about the woman he considers his muse to shame.

but the love is misplaced. it goes to people who don't really appreciate the weight of your emotions or people who constantly treat you in a manner not befitting of everything you have to offer.

this can cause you to feel a disconnect with the world.

a disconnect with the person you love and hold so dear.

a disconnect with yourself.

but to have all this potential to love is a blessing in disguise. if you can love a soul that does not deserve your love this much, imagine what more with a soul that does deserve your love?

this is not a flaw, but something so beautiful. eventually, when your love is grasped by a soul with gentle hands that understands what you have to offer, it will feel like magic. it will feel like something supernatural, as they return the waves that you emit in the manner that you have always deserved. you may be a lover of the undeserving right now, but all that love you have is a flower. a flower that a person very deserving will notice, admire, and pick up one day with no hesitance. a flower they will nurture and water every day.

"what is for you,

will come naturally.

you will find no need to force it,

no need to stress it,

it will just flow."

- billy chapata

procrastination

days just seem to go by without you attending to what you need to be attending to. the urgency to get certain things done, just doesn't feel natural and it takes everything in your body to get you off your couch, your bed or casual habitat.

but is this lack of urgency detrimental to you?

is it affecting you in ways that you realize or ways that you are completely oblivious to?

some may refer to it as being lazy, being disinterested, or being a slacker, but this is you. this is part of who you are.

you can't force yourself to do things that you don't want to do, to be more precise, you can't force yourself to do things that your soul has no interest in doing.

how is the thought of this a problem? how is it a flaw to merely feel differently about something? of course, we all have responsibilities, obligations and duties, this is the life that we have been subjected to. but that in no way means there is a problem with you taking time to do something, or you attending to something at your own time, or you not utilizing energy in something you don't want to do.

if anything, you move at your own impulses and your own vibrations. this is not a flaw, but a flower.

"there are parts to us that

we must keep secret.

not to be selfish or arrogant,

but to preserve that little bit of sanity

we have remaining."

- billy chapata

inconsiderate

feelings can be a funny thing. sometimes it's a little difficult to really understand whether we are being selfish or lacking empathy. as human beings we are so unpredictable and tricky to understand so sometimes our naivety or nonchalance to certain situations is looked down upon as something that is negative.

we're called insensitive, inconsiderate and sometimes we even feel and believe that we truly are.

but deep down, our intentions are not motivated by evil gain. it's not like our intentions are to hurt the people we love and care about.

you're human, at times there are things that you do without knowing the true magnitude of the consequences at hand. does this make you inconsiderate? or does it simply make you human?

can you really frown upon your mistakes and say on the grand scale of things that you are this inconsiderate person that has been painted? this person who doesn't care about the knock on effect of their own actions? this person who lacks a general softness and understanding of certain situations?

when you look deeper you'll see that your actions usually don't derive from a bad place. sometimes we try to do what's right and try to make sure everyone in our life is happy, and it just ends up going terribly wrong. you can't be too hard on yourself when things go wrong, and convince yourself that you're an inconsiderate person. you're human, you weren't built to be perfect. find solace in your intentions and your beautiful heart, and you'll see that this is not a flaw, but a flower.

"we run away from fear.

we run away from something

that does not even exist."

- *billy chapata*

fear

fear is an interesting thing. the funny thing about fear is that it doesn't exist. it is something that we conjure up like a magic spell in our mind after an obstacle or roadblock in our life appears. it consumes us and we start to worry about things that are not necessarily going to happen. if you think about it, and look back, a lot of the things we worry about never come to fruition, and this just shows how weak the idea of fear is.

but here you are. you find yourself scared and worrying about a situation that has not happened yet, and it is stealing your happiness and peace of mind.

it is not a bad thing to be scared.

it is not a bad thing to feel these emotions.

not knowing how something is going to turn out is a scary prospect. the thought of how something could affect you if it doesn't turn out as planned can be quite daunting.

let the oblivion be a beautiful experience. instead of worrying about what's going to happen, leave it to the universe. let the universe guide you to where you need to go. if all doesn't go to plan, know that this is a part of a bigger picture that you cannot see. eliminate that fear, and trust in your journey. trust that whatever happens is meant to happen, and it will teach you many lessons as well as grow you as an individual. let fear go, and let your flowers grow.

"honest intentions,

honest people,

honest conversations,

honest energy,

honesty is everything."

*- **billy chapata***

too honest

no one likes being lied to. as much as some people can't handle the truth, honesty is always something that frees individuals from the shackles of delusion and unawareness.

but is there ever a time when perhaps, lies would serve a better purpose?

when honesty is something that should take a backseat for the better of a situation?

if that is the case then the people in your life who feel that way do not deserve to be a part of it.

there is no such thing as being too honest. it is either you are honest or you are not. can you blame yourself for being unapologetically true to yourself and expressing how you feel? can you blame yourself for being truthful and it being taken in a manner that is not befitting of your intentions?

the ones who know you, adore you and love you, will always know that when you're being honest, it is all coming from a very good place. they will know that your honesty is intended with the idea of serving a higher and better purpose, rather than hurting and causing pain. those that don't understand this, don't understand you well enough. but what supersedes this is the knowledge that ultimately, you know yourself. honesty is beautiful, and will never be a flaw. let your flowers shine through, and do everything you do in sincerity and honesty.

"remind yourself that you're good.

if you're not,

remind yourself that it's okay

to feel what you're feeling.

embrace it,

grow from it."

- billy chapata

self-doubt

do you know your worth?

do you know what you're capable of?

do you realize your potential more than anyone around you does?

doubting yourself is natural. sometimes we reach points where we feel we have squeezed every ounce of supernatural ability in our bones to the point that we believe that we are not able to fulfill certain things or meet particular requirements.

we are human. sometimes we need that reassurance or that tap on the back that lets us know that we can do it. that reassurance that lets us know that everything will be alright.

sometimes we lose sight of ourselves in the midst's of life and the experiences we go through and the people we encounter cause us to be a little unsure about ourselves and our capabilities. it leaves us in a state where we feel frozen and feel like whatever we do will not be good enough or satisfactory.

to feel this way is not a flaw. we all fall short and stumble in our own self belief. we all reach certain points where we feel our efforts will not be rewarded with what our soul craves and our heart desires. the trick is to understand that this state of mind is a flexible one. it is one that you can change, just by understanding that what is meant to be for you will be for you, and what isn't, will not. give your full effort, give everything you have, have faith in your potential, and release that doubt. let your failures be lessons, let them help you grow, let them be your flowers.

"be true in your actions,

not perfect."

- billy chapata

perfectionist

things just have to be a certain way for you to be satisfied. if something is not how it needs to be or how it should be in your figuring, it bothers you and throws your state of mind off balance. it disturbs your sanity and causes this untraceable anxiety to consume you until you can make everything right.

your soul just doesn't feel at ease unless everything is perfect and sometimes you're even hard on yourself because you feel you can do better with certain things and certain situations.

it's hard for you to go with the flow. you need to analyze each and every step you make to make sure the steps you are taking are conducive to what you're trying to do, and this can only be achieved by making sure everything is perfect and everything is well thought out.

since when did this become such a terrible thing?

to think closely and carefully about everything and make sure that each piece to the puzzle fits in well with what the overall plan is?

to think this way shows a certain awareness that exists within you, that is rare to find. a characteristic that wants to ensure that what you're doing is done in the right manner and right fashion. some people are free spirits and some people are thinkers. this is exactly what you are, a thinker. there is nothing wrong with that. there is nothing wrong with deliberating and making sure you put in an extra effort to ensure everything runs smoothly. there is nothing wrong with setting high standards and striving for a certain level of perfection. this is not a flaw, but a flower.

"love and attachment have nothing

to do with each other.

remember that."

- billy chapata

attachment

it's hard to let go of certain things we love and adore sometimes. it's hard to release ourselves from something we have become so accustomed to over a certain period of time. it's hard to let go of a feeling that has become so familiar with us that we feel incomplete without it.

we find ourselves holding on to someone or something because we just don't want to lose it for a variety of reasons. the thought of being without that person or thing is unfathomable and one of the scariest thoughts that could ever cross your mind.

sadly, sometimes attachment causes us more problems than it actually solves. holding onto something with a tight grip can cause it to slip away right through your fingers. holding onto someone that doesn't want to be held with such intensity can cause that person to create a distance between the two of you.

we all have our reasons for attaching ourselves to people and things, and this is only normal. when you love something, you never want to lose it, so you look for any ways possible to ensure that thing stays in your life. that mere intensity and desire to ensure that the thing that brings you so much sanity and happiness stays in your life is a beautiful sentiment in itself. it is not a flaw to feel this way, but just something we have to adjust to make sure we can hold onto what we love without losing the person and a part of ourselves in the process.

love, but let them be free. attach yourself to them in spirit, and allow them to do the same, but let them wriggle free when they need. the ones that love you will always keep you close, without giving you a sense that you need to keep extra close to keep them. you will find that attachment can be a flower, that helps you understand how to treat people. don't let it be a flaw, let it be something that teaches you how to love freely.

"a beautiful woman

lets her soul speak for her.

her beauty is not defined by what

you see on the surface.

it is always much deeper than that.

- billy chapata

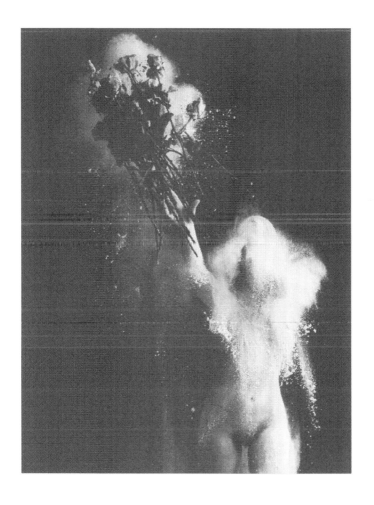

self-image

on some days you look in the mirror and feel inadequate, unattractive, ugly.

you look at your image and feel a direct disconnect with what you look like and what you feel like. a disconnect that runs deeper between who you are and what you want to be.

to feel this way on some days is natural.

there are times when our image does not reflect our true essence. days when our image sends us into a deep state of sadness, frustration or conflict. days when the mere thought of showing ourselves in public sends shivers down the spine. days when we just want to curl up into a little ball because we just don't feel our physical traits are up to scratch with where we want them to be.

there is no wrong in feeling this way. the media has built this great façade of what the perfect image is and it affects us mentally more than we think. we look at all these magazines, television shows, and movies, and think to ourselves, "this is how i'm meant to look, this is how I want to look".

understand that there is no wrong in feeling displeasure in your self-image on some days, but understand that your beauty is not measured by what you show outwards, but what you possess inwards. don't get caught up in this web of lies that the media have constructed that entails that beauty is based on image. don't be societies definition of beauty, be your own definition of beauty. be the kind of beautiful that can't be found anywhere else. the beauty that you don't see on television, movies and magazines. the raw, unaltered, unfiltered beauty. the real kind of beauty. be the rare flower that can't be found in someone else's garden.

"you can't help someone

who isn't willing to help

themselves."

- *billy chapata*

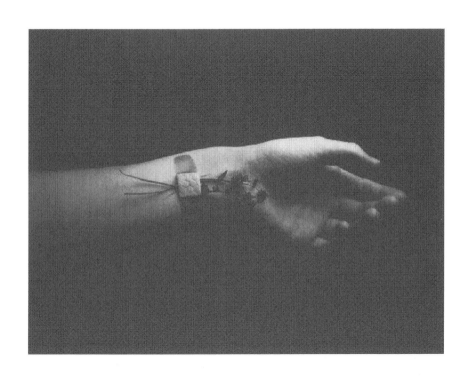

savior complex

when fires start, you're on the scene immediately. you take charge and you feel it's your responsibility to put them out.

when someone is drowning, you feel it's your responsibility to take your clothes off and dive deep down in the water to save them.

when the crowd is lost, you feel it's your responsibility to use your souls gps to guide them towards safety.

maybe at times, you don't feel it as a responsibility but something that just happens naturally. you have an inclination to assist in any situation you can because you hate to see people hurting. it pains you to see people lost with nowhere to turn.

some may point towards your actions as something that is perhaps, unnecessary or unneeded, but does that make it wrong that you find yourself indulging in these situations? situations where you jump at every opportunity to help?

there is no wrong in trying to help people, but there is also wisdom and beauty in letting people go through their situations so they can learn lessons of their own. your actions come from an unselfish place, and that in itself is beautiful. just don't find yourself inheriting other peoples pain and problems. help out when you can, but be your own savior when times are dark. be your own flower first.

"i find that while

intelligence makes you

threatening to others,

it makes you most dangerous

to yourself."

- billy chapata

too knowledgeable

wisdom.

intellectualism.

knowledge.

ingredients that are mixed in a magical beaker to create the wonderful blend that you are. you can't help but know what you know, you can't curb the depth of your mind or suit another person's intellectual level.

but can the amount of knowledge you possess be detrimental to your cause?

can you possibly become too knowledgeable for your own good?

there is nothing wrong with being knowledgeable, and there is no such thing as being too knowledgeable. those that say there is a problem or think that there is, don't deserve a piece of your mind. don't curb your intellectualism just to suit other people who can't swim in the depths of your deep mind. possessing knowledge will never be a flaw, and don't let your flowers wither away by poisoning your mind with that notion.

"don't let your kindness

breed naivety.

you want your soul to be wholesome,

you don't want your soul to be a doormat."

- billy chapata

people pleaser

this intense urge and desire to make sure the people around you are happy and satisfied.

where does it derive from?

how does it come to fruition?

is it something you choose to do for your own reasons? or does the idea of pleasing others just come naturally to you?

no one is immune to your efforts. the ones you love, your friends, and even strangers all feel your intention to make sure that they are catered to. the word "no" doesn't figure in your souls dictionary. smiles and "thank you's" are the drugs and stimulants that keep you sane, and it is all part of your journey of ensuring the ones around you are happy.

there is nothing wrong with wanting to make sure everyone's needs and wants are tended to. it is beautiful to be abundant in how considerate you are. to put people concerns before your own, is a very noble act. just always be careful not to abandon yourself in the process. as beautiful as the idea may be of pleasing another soul, it is even more beautiful to focus that energy within. flowers need their own energy to grow too.

"be gentle with her,

she's been broken before."

*- **billy chapata***

sensitive

one word can cause you to erupt,

one action can detonate you,

one thought can cause you to explode.

you find hurricanes and tornadoes brewing at the tips of your mind because of something that has been done or something that is being said. your emotions tend to get the best of you in certain situations, and the intensity you've kept tightly packed in a bottle struggles to keep inside. you can't contain how you feel, and your soul craves a release that will balance you out.

all the same, a lot people never understand it, and the general notion people make is that you're overreacting. some go further to say that you're just overlooking certain aspects in what was said or done, others just claim that you're being sensitive.

but the heart feels what the heart feels. the soul feels what the soul feels. just because others are not in tune with what you feel doesn't make it bad. just because others are not in tune with your vibrations doesn't mean you are wrong. there is no wrong in being sensitive and reacting to certain things in a way only you know how. it just shows you are in tune with your impulsions, your soul is honest, and your flowers are pure.

"it's okay to feel lost,

confused,

misunderstood.

it's okay to start over.

it's okay to try and rediscover

yourself again."

- *billy chapata*

misunderstood

as genuine, honest and sincere as we can be, sometimes the waves we emit just never flow in the same direction as everyone else. we try directing the current in the direction everything else is heading in, and we somehow manage to find ourselves off course even though the navigation system indicates that we are heading in the right direction.

we find ourselves recalibrating our inner maps in the hope of finding, or being found.

we find ourselves shouting at the top of our lungs to the point where we feel we're about to implode and wondering why nobody can hear us.

they don't get me,

they don't feel me,

they don't understand me.

with some, it's because they haven't taken the time to really understand you, and with others there just seems to be a disconnect that is hard to repair. it can cause us to feel a deep separation from people, and an even deeper disconnect with the world. but what if the problem is with them, and not with you? you vibrate on a different frequency than everyone else, and people find that hard to understand because it's something they aren't used to? something rare, something unique, something that society has painted as something that is irregular?

that is no fault of your own. it is no flaw to be the person that you are. shift your focus on understanding yourself, and worry less about the souls that misunderstand you. don't be the flower that wonders why it has different color petals compared to the other flowers in the garden, be the flower that accepts that it is different, but still blooms. be you.

"release is an important part of life.

to be able to let go of things

that have grasped your soul

and are no longer conducive,

is beautiful."

- billy chapata

letting go/releasing

life leaves us in black holes where we fall so deep into situations to the point of no return. we get sucked into these holes voluntarily and sometimes involuntarily, and struggle to find a backdoor or exit. we invest ourselves in love, in people, in relationships, friendships and ideas.

but what happens when those things we have invested so heavily in, become things that aren't conducive to your life, state of mind or general flow?

do you hold on for the sake of holding on?

or do you let go for the better good?

letting go of something you've invested so much time and energy in is a difficult process. we lose things that we feel cannot be replaced and our worlds collapse at our feet. it is only normal to find difficulty in releasing things that have a tight grip on our soul. it's hard to extinguish something that had our hearts wildly on fire. the need to hang on, is not a flaw. it reveals so much about you as a human being. the value you place in connections, the value you place in foundations, the values you place in building something sustainable. as beautiful as that notion is, understand that holding on to something that isn't conducive does you more harm than good in the long run. it puts a roadblock in between you and your growth. to progress, you need to let go, to grow, you need to let go, to evolve, you need to let go. let go, and keep a hold of yourself, turn this flaw, into a flower.

"it's okay to lose your pride over

someone you love,

but don't lose someone you love

over your pride."

- ***billy chapata***

prideful

nothing can shake you,

nothing can move you,

nothing can unhinge you.

what you believe is what you believe, and even if you agree with something someone is saying, you stick to your guns and stay glued to your opinion. you take solace in the things you say, and don't pay much attention to the words coming out of other people's mouths because you don't believe you could ever fall short of being correct.

even when you're wrong, you're right.

and when you're right, you could never be wrong.

swallowing your pride is something you hate doing, and you're not one to easily admit to defeat. you feel you're worth too much to be investing yourself in certain situations, and feel you shouldn't indulge in things that don't match your essence. you exude a certain aura about you that is unmatched, an aura that can only be grasped by people you resonate with.

it is amazing thing to take pride in your actions and your words, but pride must be used in small dosages. you must be cautious, you must be aware, you must be humble. do not overdose, because being too proud can kill even the most beautiful flowers.

"love the way you know how.

love gently if you want,

love hard if you want,

don't let anyone tell you how to love."

- billy chapata

misjudging character

what a big, wonderful heart you have.

you have the sheer ability to care for people in ways inexplicable to even the most romantic of lovers.

to care for people deeper than a mother would for her infant child.

to care for people intensely without an unwavering vibration that stays pure and consistent throughout.

you have so much beautiful energy to pour out, and pour out is exactly what you do. you shower people with affection, love and warmth. you have nothing but the kindest intentions at heart, and you believe in treating people the way you would like to be treated.

but do they reciprocate?

do they shower you back?

one of the most saddening things life can hand us are people who don't understand us. we often fall into traps of thinking that people should have the same hearts as us. the myth that they should behave in a particular manner because we act that way too. it's good to see the good in people, but it's also good to distance yourself from people who aren't conducive to your life.

it takes a while to really get it right. many will come into our lives, and many will leave, until we find the ones that are truly meant to stay.

never look at this trait of misjudging character as a flaw, look at it as an avenue of lessons. lessons on how to be gentle with your heart. lessons on not expecting too much from everyone. lessons on how you're not for everyone and how everyone is not for you. lessons on how to grow from people who don't reciprocate your love, energy and kindness. lessons on how to continue to blossom as the flower you are.

"surround yourself with more honest people. people who aren't afraid to reveal the raw truth in fear of your reaction."

- billy chapata

◯

cowardice

experiences and our environment can leave us in situations where fear consumes us with ease. we find ourselves unable to move from the place on the chess board that we are positioned on because we are being held back by this inexplicable feeling, that just doesn't seem to compute with our hearts and souls.

we dig deep, trying to understand why we feel the way we feel. why our hearts seem to skip several beats at the thought of proceeding with certain ideas and certain feelings.

it leaves us jaded, scared, stuck.

stuck in this frame of mind that seems inescapable. a prison we've formulated in our minds that doesn't allow us to progress with life. a pit that we've constructed in our mind that doesn't allow us to climb over the obstacles that appear on our paths.

to feel this way, is human, not cowardice. we all encounter phases in which our minds get the better of us. instead of being driven by confidence and ambition, we are driven by this uncontainable fear that inhibits our soul and stops us from doing what we're supposed to do or what we want to do. at times we fear the consequences, the results, the what ifs.

do not be ashamed of this, but rather see it as way to brighten your petals up and bring out even more vibrant colors in your arsenal. see it as a way to grow from a dark place into a bright place that your leaves can catch light from. to be scared is not a flaw. you are no coward, you are human. be compassionate with yourself and keep blossoming.

"blind loyalty

will lead you

into a dark

cave of confusion."

*- **billy chapata***

drowning confusion

at times we find our minds drowning themselves in a deep well full of thoughts, memories and emotions. a situation which leaves our brains struggling to get air.

a situation that seems never ending.

a situation that appears out of nothing.

a situation that is never any fault of your own.

we're left with more questions than answers, more queries than solutions, more ideas than applications. we find that we can't seem to grasp the actions of the people around us and the demons that we seem to battle within. it sends us into a state of conflict which leaves us confused.

life is a puzzle, in which pieces that look like they're supposed to fit don't fit sometimes, so it's only natural to feel confused during certain seasons and periods in our lives. we look for clarity in different things but at the end of the day our vision never ceases being muddy and fuzzy.

it's okay to feel puzzled and conflicted within, because the universe has a way of constantly rearranging our paths to the point where we can't make sense of anything any more. trust more in your journey, and be more accepting to things you don't understand. there is always a reason behind everything that occurs in our lives, and time makes sense of it all. be patient, realize your confusion is no flaw, but a state of awareness. you need things to make sense, you're searching for answers, you want peace of mind. this is beautiful.

"think of your energy in a cup.

you give it out, the cup empties.

the goal is to interact with people that refill that cup.

reciprocation."

- billy chapata

too caring

empathy is admirable. sometimes we can't help but nurture and love the things and people around us. we find ourselves giving all this love and affection away free of charge, not asking for much in return. our affection comes with no conditions or hidden agendas, but for some reason it's never enough to provide us peace. we somehow manage to find ourselves on the bad end of the stick.

people have a habit of taking affection for granted, and they tend not to appreciate all these traits we seem to encompass. sometimes what we find in the most painful and hurtful manner, is that the love and affection we have to give always comes back to bite us.

it leaves us wondering;

do i give too much?

do i care too much?

but in reality, there isn't really anything wrong with caring too much. it shows your beauty as a person, your concern for things that may not even deserve your concern. it shows the lack of judgment you encompass in your bones and your ability to show love in the darkest moments. don't let anyone tell you that there is such a thing as caring too much.

sometimes we care for the wrong people and assume we care too much, when in essence, we were just caring for someone undeserving of all we have.

once you direct all that care to someone who does deserve it, they will appreciate you and you will blossom as a result. to care, is not a flaw. if only more people in the world cared as much as you do.

"on some days,

i believe in communication,

on other days i believe in silence.

in between the two,

i exist."

- ***billy chapata***

communication

when silence becomes your best friend.

when no one else understands, silence understands.

when you can't express yourself, silence expresses itself for you.

when no one else is around, silence is there for you.

we find at times that communication is something that becomes non-existent because of the way we are as people or because past experiences have made us believe less in communication.

we stand firm in our quietness and let our silence do the work. at times, we're just incapable of spilling out nuances and sentences that wouldn't break into a hot exchange of words or an argument. at other times we feel like our expression is just never understood when we express how we feel or what we want, so the best solution is not saying anything at all.

communication is key in any relationship, friendship or connection, but communication isn't everything. sometimes silence has a more powerful effect that leaves a more lasting impression on your counterpart. not because you are trying to be malicious, but just because silence has the ability to speak louder than words. communication is important, silence is important too, find a balance between the two, and you will be the flower that grows from concrete.

"some deserve your vulnerability,

and others deserve to be met with

an impenetrable shell.

there's nothing wrong with protecting

your aura."

- billy chapata

overly guarded

for some of us, our rib cages are heavily reinforced with metal plates and spikes that stops any intruders from finding a way through. anyone who does find a way through, is met with an assertive and aggressive defense mechanism that pushes anyone who comes close, further and further away.

we guard ourselves,

we guard our energy,

we guard our hearts from anyone that looks and feels like the enemy.

this only comes with its fair share of critics or self resentment that makes us feel like we're too guarded. people who attempt to get closer to us are the ones who release the loudest cries. the ones who try by all means to find a way into our hearts or try to understand us are the ones who feel like the harshest victims.

but is there really a problem with protecting your space?

absolutely not.

there is nothing wrong with running away or distancing yourself from something that feels like danger. there is nothing wrong with putting yourself first and making sure your heart is well protected. there is nothing wrong with having a love for yourself and general care for your heart. there is no wrong with defending that until someone who can open all your defenses gently, comes along and makes the wait worth it. this is not a flaw, but a flower.

"don't let the past dictate you.

keep loving like a tidal wave

and eventually you'll find someone

who already knows how to swim."

- billy chapata

too sentimental

looking back at memories can become a favorite past time.

reminiscing on all of the sweet times and rewinding the clocks can become addictive.

sometimes, we can't help but find ourselves digging deep into our hearts archive and library, and replaying videos in our mind of all the times we shared with family, friends and lovers, despite the fact that some of the times may have left us numb.

we think of who we think of,

we miss who we miss.

there are some things that cannot be avoided, and certain sentiments find themselves inscribed on our souls like a permanent tattoo for a very long time. it's only natural to take trips down memory lane, sometimes visits of the past can be a release and cathartic.

memories can be beautiful, but be sure to make new memories with new people. dwelling on the past can hinder our growth and stop us from progressing. being sentimental is not a flaw, but rather an indication at your value of connections. you cherish the beautiful times, and shed tears at the bad times you had with people at one point in your life, there is no wrong in that. sometimes experiences are what help us to be the strong flower we need to be for ourselves, and sometimes memories are what help us bloom to become the beautiful flower we need to be in the future.

"love and action go hand in hand.

professing your love with no

resonating actions behind your words,

makes your claims useless."

- *billy chapata*

gullible

we are drawn into certain things, and gravitate towards certain energy. at times we have no hesitation in giving in to that magnetic pull, and have no hesitation in believing the things that we are being given or being told.

sometimes we can't help but believe what people are feeding us, and it only leads us to feel very upset. it leaves us kicking ourselves wondering why we would believe what was being presented to us in the first place.

why was i so naive?

why did i believe everything i was told, without thinking a little deeper?

why do i fall for things so easily?

this is no fault of your own. there is an innocence about you that finds itself latching onto the idea that everyone is good and has your best interests at hand. sadly, we come across so many characters in life that are able to manipulate emotions, truths and feelings without having an ounce of regret. for you to give people the benefit of the doubt and believe the things being said is not a flaw. the trick is to be a little more patient with people and let them reveal their true colors before believing everything they say and do. understand them better, but understand yourself more. question more and accept less. create a balance. don't do one more than the other. be more aware, and blossom.

"at one point in time,

something you love and cherish

will cut you,

leaving a deep wound.

it's all about finding something

worth bleeding for."

- ***billy chapata***

reckless lover

have you ever felt like a magnet to the universe?

the feeling of having a "feel good" mutuality with the stars?

there are times when we seem to attract beautiful things. we become a giant human magnet that brings in all these things that present themselves to us in a manner that almost seems effortless. a beautifully wrapped gift made just for us.

we find these things giving us so much affection and putting all the emotions they feel for us in a jar and placing it directly in our palms, but we always seem to find a way to drop the jar, breaking all the things that were built up, and seemingly destroying the true essence of the connection or love that was built.

our past tends to make us reckless with love, and sometimes we can't seem to quite grasp the warmth of the love the same way we used to. the people who come into our life are the ones who suffer the consequences. we just can't seem to take care of beautiful things and let our past experiences interfere in our nurturing process.

all the bad things that have happened to you in the past cannot all be attributed to you. what needs to be done is a real reflection. learn from the past. learn to love yourself, because when you don't love yourself, you are incapable of loving another soul. let go of all the memories of past relationships or connections and grow from them. be more gentle. be the flower that has been nurtured. the flower that has no thorns on its sides, the flower that has learnt from pain and is ready to give it out.

"there is nothing wrong with

feeling vulnerable.

allow yourself to feel everything.

absorb the pain,

understand it,

heal yourself.

- *billy chapata*

open heart

we don't all have defense mechanisms. for some of us, the idea of backing into a corner and putting our guards up is foreign. the idea of resistance doesn't seem to exist. we allow ourselves to be open to the worlds energy and open our heart out to different energies, vibrations and people.

as someone with an open heart, you may be receptive to most of the things life and people have to offer. as amazing as it may seem to the outside, it can cause a huge conflict within you because you don't know whether you're the artist of your own demise.

by leaving yourself open, do you invite people to betray you?

do you invite people to hurt you?

do you invite people to lie to you?

it can cause you to feel a disconnect between your emotions, and leave you questioning whether your stance is doing you more harm than good.

there is no wrong with leaving yourself open. vulnerability is a great sign of bravery and courage. to leave yourself more open to people and ideas is beautiful, and more people should exude these kinds of traits. protect yourself when you need to protect yourself, but continue to be open. a flower can only grow, when it is removed from the dark box that it is placed in, and exposed to the light, air and soil. take pride in your openness, it is not a flaw.

"trust your intuition,

we feel things for a reason."

- *billychapata*

too trusting

sometimes we find it easy to place a part of ourselves in another person's hands. we find hands that feel warm, forgetting that even the warmest hands can turn cold. we give people the benefit of the doubt without over-thinking it too much. our beliefs in people can be unprecedented, and that belief comes with its own share of problems that affects us deeper than a lot of people really understand.

sometimes we find that our belief in people always finds a way to come back and bite us, and we attribute everything that happens to being too trusting of people.

our acts of love, loyalty and affection repaid with lying, deceit and dishonesty. an unfair trade. it is a trade that can leave the deepest scars in an individual's heart, and leave one never being able to trust again.

there is no wrong, in being too trusting of people, but it is something you must learn from. take solace in the fact that you are open to giving people chances to prove their loyalty but also be aware that people don't always mean what they say or promise. give chances, but be cautious. be wise, be observant, be a little analytical. you're a flower, and you can't allow everyone's hands to touch your petals. not everyone has your best interests at heart.

"ever felt restless?

ever felt an itch deep down in your soul,

something indescribable?"

  - billy chapata

restless

our minds are more complex and complicated than we give them credit for. they are running even when we don't think they are running. they are working even when we think they aren't. at times, our minds, hearts and souls can't seem to sit still. no matter how hard we try, we find it difficult to contain all the bursts of anxiety we feel flow through our blood and veins.

it could be the mere anticipation of something, or the oblivion of not knowing what is going to happen next that sends us into this uncontrollable state.

you want a resolution,

you want a solution,

you want answers.

you want something that will liberate and free your soul. it brings you to a place where you find it hard to cope with certain situations, and a place where you start becoming upset and even frustrated with yourself.

it's natural to feel restless. it just shows that your mind is always moving, your mind is always ticking, your mind is always active, it shows that you're alive. restlessness is a plea from your soul for freedom. something that can only stop once your soul gets what it desires. the soul wants what the soul wants, and until then, the restlessness will ensue. take a few deep breaths, relax, and don't think too far ahead. think about the now, and what will give you joy now. leave the worries and expectations of tomorrow that cause you to feel restless. your mind needs to inhale and exhale. flowers need to breathe too.

"someone out there appreciates

your flaws."

*- **billy chapata***

self hatred

when you look in the mirror, what do you see?

when you focus your energy inwards and analyze all your traits and behaviors, what do you conclude about yourself?

everything you do and everything you comprise of is a unique part of who you are. something that nobody else can possess or even try to emulate. something that nobody can steal from you or imitate.

but here you are.

you find yourself hating the beautiful parts that make you, you. all because society has told you and shown you that what you are is not what is acceptable.

you are not worthy because you exude a certain persona?

you are not beautiful because you don't look a certain way?

you look at yourself and find yourself lacking the image that displays itself in your favorite magazines or your most addictive television shows, but you're more than that. you're more divine than that, simply because you are real. you are not something concocted on a screen or written in print, you are something that really exists. turn that hate you have for yourself into love, because that's what you deserve - love. not love from another soul, but love from yourself. love creates flowers, and hate destroys them. love yourself.

"you may say or do

the wrong things sometimes,

but that doesn't mean your heart isn't

coming from a good place."

- *billy chapata*

indecisive

sometimes, we find ourselves in these deep entanglements between what we want and what we need. we can never really seem to make up our mind as to what takes priority in our soul. decisions and resolutions never seem to stick and we find ourselves putting our choices on a merry go round of emotions.

whenever something seems right, we turn around and feel it couldn't be more wrong.

whenever something seems wrong, we turn around and feel it couldn't be more right.

it may be brought about by a feeling of being unsure, or maybe it's just brought about by a series of over-thinking. what remains true is the fact that we can never really seem to make our minds up about certain things. we find our hearts, our minds and our souls coming to collisions while trying to figure out and balance out the correct options.

there is no wrong in being indecisive, it just shows how analytical you are and how you are always striving to make the right decisions. many go with the wind and don't really think about what they are indulging in and what they are exposing themselves to. you assess your options carefully and don't mind taking the time to make sure the choice you're going with is the best one forward. that's beautiful and it always will be.

"your energy is not to be understood by everyone.

your energy is not to be shared with everyone."

- billy chapata

evasive

often times, we find ourselves running away from people and situations that we're trying to avoid. we run for miles and days trying to find our safe zones, jumping over obstacles, skipping over gaps, and climbing over walls just so we won't have to face situations and people.

we do it for different reasons.

sometimes we do it because we're trying to avoid confrontation, and other times we do it because we just can't be bothered with indulging in pointless, or draining interactions with people that don't matter that much to us. nonetheless, we find ourselves in situations where we just don't want to be near anything or anyone.

but is the idea of trying to find an escape really a bad thing?

is the idea of being evasive really a flaw?

there is no wrong in trying to avoid things that you do not want to interact with.

there is no wrong in avoiding ideas that you do not want to indulge in.

there is no wrong in distancing yourself from poisonous connections and people.

some may look at it as a cowardly thing to do, but there is so much bravery and wisdom in knowing when to separate yourself from a situation or a person. it is not a flaw to be evasive. it is only a beautiful thing to know what is for you and what is not for you.

"you can't beat yourself up for

having too much love to give.

you can only feel sorry for those

who don't know what they're missing

out on."

- billy chapata

<u>over-lover</u>

where does all the love you have to give go?

where does all the love that you have to give end up?

you have all this love to give but somehow your love seems to end up in the hands of souls that can't grasp the full entirety of what you have to offer. you love so hard to the point that the ones who receive all your warmth get burnt by the intensity of what you have to offer. you love so hard that the ones who you have such a tight grip on always seem to slip right through your fingers and disappear from your very eyes like a magic trick.

you're left with questions wondering what's wrong with you?

what am i doing wrong?

why do i have so much love to give?

being an over-lover is not a flaw. to have an abundance of love to spread out is something many cannot do because the past has left them incapable of doing so. take pride in your ability to love with such passion, don't let anyone tell you that you love too much. a flower needs love to grow, and as long as you have that for yourself first, you will never stop blossoming.

"a true soul mate will always

have clear intentions.

their actions and words will

always reassure you that your

love is in a safe place."

- billy chapata

insecure

at times, we can never seem to feel safe. there always seems to be something that lurks in the background of our minds, casting doubt on the things we felt so sure about before. it starts off as a little seed and sprouts into something much bigger. something that is hard to control and contain.

we're not sure why, but we just can't help but feel this uneasiness about a particular thing or a particular person. it causes us to feel this deep unrest within our souls and we start to behave out of character. it consumes us so much to the point that we start to raise assumptions about things we are unsure about, and in some cases, even forces us to lash out at a particular thing or person, for something that they may not even be guilty of in the first place.

the insecurity swallows us into a place of delusion and stress. we start worrying about things that are not even taking place. things that we have magically created in our heads.

be the flower that knows it's worth.

there is no reason why a divine creature such as yourself should be constantly battling emotions that concern your insecurity about a person or a particular thing. when you know your worth, you'll know what you have to offer. the things other people do, won't concern you as much as the things you are doing yourself. don't let insecurity kill your flowers. let it be something you can grow from and learn from. understand your value and what you have to offer. you are beautiful.

"don't dwell on the what if's

and could have been's.

where you are right now is

where you need to be.

trust in the timing of the universe.

- billy chapata

hopeless

there just seems to be no way to get out of this dead end, and you're not too sure where you are going to turn. a huge traffic jam that doesn't seem to cease, with no routes and exits to escape on to. it seems like everything you try never comes to fruition and you start to feel like there really isn't a point to everything you are trying to accomplish. everything you touch seems to crumble, and everything you manage to get your hold on melts away.

you get the feeling that everything you put in doesn't yield the desired effect that you intended. you start to feel an emptiness in your soul, like somebody carved a deep hole in your chest with a box cutter, leaving it wide open and prone to the elements.

it's normal to feel this way in certain situations. we are human, and we tend to let out past mistakes haunt our future. at times we fail once and believe that we are doomed to fail over and over again. instead of just giving it a shot again, we get disheartened and feel like the best way forward is not to try again at all. rise against it. be the flower that isn't afraid to try. the flower that isn't afraid of growth. turn hopelessness into a state of hope and let that be your flower. let it be the flower that always reminds you that no matter how tough things can get at times, there is always a way.

"sometimes, it's important not to

interrupt someone else's healing process.

don't inherit all their dirt,

and all their pain,

and hurt yourself in the process."

- billy chapata

empathetic

it's rare to find people these days that genuinely put themselves in another person's position and truly allow themselves to feel what they feel. people that allow themselves to embrace someone else's pain, struggle and heartache. there simply aren't enough selfless people who care for other people situations.

for you on the other hand, it's not hard for you to put yourself in another person's shoes. no matter how big or small the shoes are, you always find a way to make sure they fit on your feet.

instead of looking at things from a more individualistic perspective, you look at things from a more selfless point of view and can't help but try to find an understanding, or help a person who is going through hardship. sometimes it leaves you in tricky situations because you find yourself being empathetic towards people who don't deserve your empathy, and it leaves you torn.

there is no wrong in being empathetic, and there is no such thing as being too empathetic. to put yourself in another person's position and to feel what they feel, takes great courage, great bravery and great selflessness. take pride in your ability to feel. in your ability to see another person as human. someone who makes mistakes, someone who gets hurt, someone who suffers pain, and someone who has lows. it's beautiful to have understanding, and a beautiful flower to possess.

"choose to be happy.

if that means keeping

to yourself and ignoring

those that drain your energy,

so be it.

just choose to be happy."

- *billy chapata*

withdrawn

distance and solitude are often misunderstood. at times we find comfort in being alone. we don't really see the need to socialize much, and we feel a strong vibration throughout our souls that wants us to be reclusive.

we'd rather not talk,

not listen,

not interact.

what resonates the most with us is being alone and enjoying our own company. time alone, where we can escape the noise and distractions from the outside world. we're all about our own growth and our inner energy. we can't seem to sum up the energy and passion in our bones to change that aspect of ourselves, and we tend to distance ourselves from people who can't understand that.

we have very few companions and this is because the best companion we have, is ourselves. we find home within ourselves and everything else is foreign. being withdrawn is never a problem especially when you find your joy from being away from everyone. when you find comfort in being by yourself you have found the greatest key one can find;

comfort.

when you're comfortable with yourself, you enhance the energies of the people around you and that is one of the most beautiful things you can do. don't look at being withdrawn as a flaw, because it is not. look at it as being an analytical person who spots the bad things that could happen, and making a conscious decision to stay away. a flower that knows when to show its petals when needed, and a flower that knows when to put them away when required.

"the goal is not drown them in love.

it's to give them love they can dive in,

come up for air,

and swim freely in.

a boundless kinda love."

- billy chapata

unattached

life brings us to points where we find ourselves in connections, that don't seem to connect to us. our souls, our minds and our hearts can never seem to grasp the depth of what we are swimming in.

not because of the lack of effort,

or the lack of wanting,

but just because there is a natural lack of desire to attach ourselves to anything or anyone. you can't force yourself to feel what others around you want you and expect you to feel. sometimes it forces us to think that there is a problem with us, or that there is something that we may be doing wrong, when in actuality we are just victims of being misunderstood.

there is nothing wrong with feeling this way.

feeling unattached is not a flaw, but rather just a natural vibration that resonates within. sometimes we don't like being chained to ideas, people and emotions, and there is no wrong in that. it's a blessing to be able to unhook yourself from certain things, and when you do find something that you feel connected to, you will always have the ability to leave it alone when things get bad.

"some people deserve to be in your life,

and some people don't.

it's all about finding the right balance."

- *billy chapata*

hypocritical

we have this habit of finding this very refined distaste in the behavior and actions of other people. we're not quite sure why but we find ourselves finding fault in a lot of the things people do and say.

they're never quite right in their standards, and we expect a little better from them. we expect them to behave in a manner befitting the standards we have subconsciously concocted in our mind for them.

but flip the coin, and fast forward to a time later on, and you find yourself doing the exact same things that you frowned upon. you become that very thing that you hate so much. and you're not quite sure why, but you find yourself falling into the same hole that everyone you criticized fell into.

we are all hypocritical at one point in time.

we are human.

sometimes our actions are out of pure reaction rather than thought, and until we sit down and analyze everything we have done, we never realize that we have done the exact same thing that we vowed never to do. accept that you'll make mistakes, but do not be judgmental of others mistakes. let your mistakes be your mistakes to grow from, and let their mistakes be their mistakes to grow from. focus on you, and less on everyone else. be about your growth, be about your journey, be about you.

"some thoughts are meant to be free,

and some thoughts are meant to be handcuffed

to the frame of your mind until the time is right."

- billy chapata

uptight and anxious

feeling this tense uncontrollable anxiety.

this anxiety that can't be summed in words but by the mere fact that you seem to be in a state of mind that leaves you on the cusp of reacting to something in an unfamiliar way. you find yourself being overly sensitive to the things people say and do, and you can't help but lash out in a way that you don't understand after a period of time.

lashing out is almost a defense mechanism of sorts, that defends you from the actions of other people. your anxiety plays up to the point that you feel that there is a real need to be defensive and careful of all the things people are saying and doing. others around you don't quite understand your behavior and even question why you behave the way you do, showing signs of frustration and confusion.

but this is you.

this is just a part of who you are.

being uptight is not a flaw, but something that you can grow from. the reason you feel the way you feel, is no fault of your own, but a result of the things that have happened in the past.

things that have transformed you into the person you are now.

look at it as a way to grow. you can't experience new things if you're not a little more easy going about things. relax, be patient, breathe, take in new things, new people, new experiences. you cannot grow by staying in your comfort zone. you can't grow by always accepting what you're accustomed to, and rejecting what you're not familiar with. open your petals up, allow butterflies to land on them, and blossom into a flower that is open to the elements of the world.

"we don't crave people,

we crave the feelings they give us,

the way they make us feel."

- billy chapata

feeling too much

sometimes soft blows hit us like oversized trucks speeding on the highway.

we feel things on a deeper level than we probably should,

but nonetheless, we still feel.

these things strike us right at the core, and the feelings just seem to overwhelm us to the point where our emotions get the best of us. we find ourselves drowning in these emotions, struggling for air, with no lifeguard on duty.

at times, we try to block these emotions, but the superhero instincts we possess never seem to get the better of how we feel.

it is no crime to feel.

there is no such thing as feeling too much.

you feel what you feel for a reason, and sometimes there is no reason to question it.

embrace what you feel because there is a reason why you're feeling it. whether you feel it too much, or feel it a little less than usual, doesn't make it right or wrong. your impulses and intuition are your strongest guide in the universe, and if you want to bloom into something indestructible, sometimes you have to follow those inclinations.

"sometimes we just have to accept

and not question.

sometimes we just have to

go with the flow."

- ***billy chapata***

stubborn

you can't take no for an answer and you have your suspicions when you're given yes as an answer. you question everything, and reject many. it seems to be a natural part of your essence and it is something that describes you perfectly.

your stubbornness is unmatched and you simply cannot take everything everyone says without having your slight doubts. when doubt does occur, you find yourself speaking out without hesitation and rejecting the ideas people bring into the universe.

stubbornness is not a bad thing.

it just shows that you are unwilling to accept everything that is handed to you, and that you handle everything that is given to you with caution. you make things a little hard for people, but it is a process that weeds out the people who aren't patient with you, and remove those that aren't willing to accept you the way you are. being stubborn is not a flaw, but understand that it is a beautiful thing to know when to accept things. find the balance between stubbornness and being accepting, and you will blossom into something quite incredible.

don't let them poison your aura

with false opinions and assumptions.

keep your soul vibrant with reminders

of yourself worth."

- ***billy chapata***

self worth

do you value yourself?

do you value what you have to offer?

when you focus your energy inwards do you fall in love with what you see?

or do you feel a deep dissatisfaction with what you see?

life leaves us in situations that has forgetting what we're worth, and how much we're worth. we base our worth on what people feel about us rather than what we feel about ourselves. other people's ideas leave us feeling empty and we abandon the ideas that we should be concerning ourselves with.

never measure you worth by other people's ideas and standards.

once you do, you sell yourself short and undervalue your true essence.

understand that you are a beautiful being, that cannot be compared to anything else on this planet. your value and your worth are priceless, and cannot be replaced by anything. anyone who doesn't understand that, does not deserve to be a part of your circle of energy. know when to walk away from the people who don't know your worth, know when to remove the people who devalue you, and know when to gravitate towards those who cherish your presence and understand what you have to offer. take pride in your essence, your aura, and who you are.

":your energy is not always

going to compliment everyone else's,

and that's only natural.

gravitate towards the vibes that suit you."

- billy chapata

nonchalance

you can't be bothered by the things around you. you carry yourself in a manner that almost makes it seem as if you don't care, or only care about things pertaining to you. one would be mistaken to think that you lack awareness and that you just go with the flow without putting much into your actions,

but there is a deeper layer that they haven't quite been able to decode.

your mood is always very toned down, and you never seem to be enthusiastic about things concerning other people. avoiding situations and people because you feel it will affect your energy, is part of the norm, but those around you mistake your nonchalance for a lack of concern or selfishness.

there is no wrong in being nonchalant.

there is no wrong in focusing all your energy on yourself and choosing to distance yourself from things that don't concern you. more people should adopt the idea of only interacting with people when it is absolutely needed, and stop gravitating towards things that they don't need to. there is no need to drain your energy interacting in things and people that you don't want to interact with.

"never leave yourself unattended.

as you spread your energy into the universe,

never forget to invest in yourself."

- *billy chapata*

selfless

do you put everyone's emotions and feelings before your own?

do you leave yourself unattended while everyone around you is fulfilled?

sometimes we give more than we receive. we put other people before ourselves, neglecting the very divine structure and temple that we are. feeding them while we starve, serving them while we work, loving them while we aren't appreciated.

it's a natural part of who you are. you give so much, while forgetting that you need to recover as well to maintain a balance. a balance that allows you to reenergize yourself, a balance that doesn't drain the marrow out of your bones and leave you weak, and on your knees.

a balance that makes you feel like a human being and not an emotional slave.

it's a beautiful thing to be selfless, but it is also a very dangerous thing too. reciprocation is very important. don't indulge in one sided connections. water each other, support each other, be available to each other. create a balance and mutual understanding that leaves you both satisfied mentally and spiritually. it is not a flaw to be selfless, but an indication of how beautiful and unselfish you are. a flower that would give its roots away to ensure the flowers around them grow. just don't forget that you need to grow and be nurtured too.

"everyone you interact with brings

out a different side to you.

the goal is to keep the ones who bring out

the beautiful parts to you."

- billy chapata

compartmentalize

"he belongs here" because he looks like this.

"she belongs there" because she behaves like this.

"they don't do this" because they don't look like the type.

"we need to do more of that" because we are looking like a certain type of way to our peers.

you find yourself dividing things and people into certain imaginary categories that you can't explain. you do it subconsciously without noticing. you do it because it makes you feel much more comfortable to know that people belong in certain groups, and it makes you feel like it will help you understand them better, or help you understand how to approach situations.

compartmentalizing is something everyone does from time to time without knowing. grouping people into certain categories because of their gender, lifestyle or looks. however, doing this is a false representation of people because there is much more to everyone than those simple things.

look deeper,

treat everyone as an equal.

regardless of the past experiences you may have encountered, realize that everyone is different and unique in their own way and thus, must be treated with the same respect. be wise with your approach, and treat everyone like a different unique experience. a true test of a flower is its ability to survive different seasons and different conditions.

"be aware of your environment

and the things around you.

be aware of the people in your life

and how they make you feel."

- billy chapata

self conscious

from time to time, we constantly pick apart different facets to ourselves that we dislike and it leaves us in a dark place.

a place which you find hard to move from,

a place that makes you feel trapped.

we find it hard to go out, hard to be ourselves, and hard to interact with others because we feel like we're lacking the necessary ingredients to mix with the other people in the pot. we look at ourselves and feel like we're missing that something extra. that extra thing that gives us the confidence and wave to go out there and expose ourselves to the world and its inhabitants.

there is nothing wrong with feeling self conscious.

we're all a little self conscious in our own ways.

just do not let the idea of yourself consume you so much to the point that you swallow yourself into a dark pit that you cannot escape from. understand that the only impression you need to leave, is on yourself. no one else's opinion matters, but your own. understand this, and you will blossom into something truly unbreakable.

"even the wrong decisions can

breed the right outcomes.

trust your process. trust your journey."

- billy chapata

fear of the future

mental views into the future.

taking the mental telescope out from one of the shelves in your heart,

placing it on the edge of your mind,

and gazing into the future.

looking into the future can be a scary prospect. one that scares even some of the most bravest and resilient souls into a place that they do not want to return from. the future can present its fair share of obstacles that we predict happen even before we really know the true outcome.

we find ourselves stressing and fearing things that haven't happened,

things that don't fall into accordance with our goals and dreams,

things that we feel could affect our lives, and the people around us.

fearing the future is only natural. the future is unknown, and fear of the unknown is common. but that's the beauty of it all. the general oblivion of it. there is no fun in knowing how everything should be set out. be more spontaneous in your approach. let things map themselves out and go with the flow. instead of being scared of your future, grab a hold of it, and make it yours. set a foundation that you dictate. a foundation that you can be excited about. a foundation that leaves you hopeful, intrigued and less fearful.

"be with someone who understands your love,

reciprocates your love,

cherishes your love,

and accepts it."

- *billy chapata*

too naive

you appear to be easy going about things and tend to put weight in people's words. you don't put much thought into the things people say and do, and tend to just go with the flow. you see the good in people, so the words that come from their lips seem to be gospel. you believe that people have your best interests.

you have an innocence about you, particularly in your thought process, and a pureness in the way you view life and people.

sadly,

you always find yourself in deep water with your state of mind and the way you view things. people seem to betray your loyalty and trust in their words and actions. you feel hurt in the way people treat your kindness, your softness and your vulnerability, and yearn for a reciprocation in the way you treat others.

being naive can be bliss, in the sense that you don't concern yourself in things that you don't need to concern yourself in, but always remember to be aware. be more aware in the way you view situations, people and ideas. think things through carefully, understand better, and treat people accordingly. understand yourself better in order to understand others better. be the flower that understands it's strengths and weaknesses.

"breathe a little.

don't let life consume you.

don't miss out on life because you're

inhaling too much of it.

exhale and cherish the moments."

- *billy chapata*

overindulgence

you put in more and more,

over and over again.

you put your soul in the cusp of your palm and open your palm to the world. you can't seem to get enough of your vice, your addiction, your favorite past time.

you indulge in the things you enjoy the most, knowing at the back of your mind that continuing to indulge in those same things could lead to your demise. you attempt to do things in moderation but find yourself indulging deeper and deeper, and unable to contain the vibrations and impulses you feel.

why do you continue to give in?

why do you continue to indulge?

everything should be done in balanced quantities and that is something you must always remember. as good as something is, or as amazing as something may feel, you never want to overindulge in it, because that kills the beauty and intrigue of it. keep it special, keep it rare, keep it untainted, keep it beautiful.

"your words have the ability to linger

in the corners of someone's mind,

and in the depths of their soul.

choose them wisely."

- *billy chapata*

verbally harsh

you have the tongue of a viper and the impulses of a scorpion.

it doesn't take much to set you off, and cause a volcano to erupt from within. this results in you having some unkind words for the people who rub you off the wrong way.

the ferocity that your mouth works at, burns down even the most solid and stable of structures, and leaves ashes and rubble at the tip of your feet. you exude a verbal hotness that could melt the biggest of icebergs in antarctica.

after the fury subsides, you feel a sense of sympathy for the victim of your fury, and a deep regret in the way you express yourself. there is no wrong in expressing yourself verbally, but always remember that;

it is not how intensely you express yourself,

but how effectively you do it.

being harsh, and expressing yourself in a verbal fury, is not always the most precise way to get a point across, and at times, makes issues even worse. sometimes a more subtle approach gets the point across better. sometimes people understand things when we present things in a softness that allows them to feel comfortable, safe, and human. be wise in your approach, be wise in your expression. be a wise flower.

"it's better to drop

your own walls,

than to wait for

someone to break them down.

there's beauty in patience

and courage in vulnerability."

- billy chapata

fear of being vulnerable

sometimes we are left with this unshakable feeling. a feeling that leaves us in a state of mind where we feel like we can't let go and release from the clutches of the world.

we put solid metal shields around our hearts and make sure our souls are covered with a protective material that no one can penetrate. we do it for a variety of reasons and feel justified in the way we do it.

at times it's the past that causes us to activate our defenses,

at times it's the experiences we see our peers going through,

and at other times it's just the fear of having to go through something or feel something that doesn't seem desirable.

whatever the case may be, being afraid of being vulnerable is a natural thing. many have built walls around their hearts in the aim of keeping intruders out, and there is nothing wrong with that. but there is no harm in letting through those that make a conscious effort to understand you.

those that still appreciate you and love you even though the walls have stayed up in all their time of knowing you.

there is no harm in letting the walls down to let certain people in.

there is no harm in allowing some to admire your petals, your colors, and the way you bloom.

"take your time with life.

observe slowly,

experience everything,

feel it all,

take it in,

breathe."

- billy chapata

impulsive

you react to everything around you.

not because you force yourself to react, but just because it is a natural process and part of who you are. it could be the smallest thing, or the most intense and serious of things, regardless, it never fails to get a reaction out of you.

you move with the vibrations and feed off energy, and this breeds your impulses. when something doesn't feel right, or something feels out of place, your soul opens itself up and you attach yourself to the issue quickly without hesitance. you address what needs to be addressed with a reaction. it may be verbal or physical, but what remains true, is the fact that your impulses never cease to react, and you jump at the opportunity to reveal how you feel about a lot of situations.

this part to you feels completely unforced, unfabricated and unhinged.

you react the way you react and there is no helping it.

it's a beautiful thing to move by impulse but also a dangerous thing too. take a few deep breaths, calm yourself, and analyze the situation before reacting. not every situation deserves a reaction, and sometimes a more calm, mellow outlook, solves and avoids any potential problems. know when to react, and know when to keep calm. be the flower that understands that sometimes, the least brightest and vibrant flower in the garden, is the one that can catch the attention more.

"let your intuition guide you,

not your ego."

- *billy chapata*

ego

your opinion of yourself is incomparable.

you believe you are great, and you live like you are.

it's in the way you walk, the things you speak about, and the way you behave. your opinion of yourself takes precedence over the opinion others may have about you, and if others have a high opinion of you, you use that as fuel to ignite your ego.

you take offence in the things people say to you, unless it's something that resonates with your greatness. small things that people say to you that don't feel right, hurt your essence and aura, and you lash out in an effort to defend your honor and pride.

while it is beautiful to take pride in yourself and the things you may have to offer, you must be wary that the very thing that you show off so much, can be the same thing that destroys you.

your ego can be a dangerous thing because it can have you feeling higher than you actually are. taking you miles into the clouds with no parachute and safety net down below in case you begin to drop.

be humble in your approach to life.

a little ego, and pride in what you do is beautiful, but an overdose on that, and it becomes poisonous to you. don't feed on that poison. let your flowers be pure in their growth, and don't feed on anything that stops them from blossoming.

keep
growing,
keep
blossoming.

ॐ

Made in the USA
San Bernardino, CA
12 September 2017